By the Pleasing Countenance of My Superiors

The life of Dungog Magistrate Thomas Cook, J.P.

now including

This anomalous community

Dungog Magistrates' Letterbook, 1834-1839.

The estate of Thomas Cook, Auchentorlie, near Dungog from the *Illustrated Sydney News*, August 5th, 1854

by Michael Williams

By the Pleasing Countenance of My Superiors,
including *This anomalous community*

Second edition, September 10, 2024.

ISBN: 979-8-227-45334-1

Written by Michael Williams.

Published by *ChideStudy Press*

For inquires or to order copies email:

ChidestudyPress@gmail.com

Website: chidestudypress.com.au

Chidestudy
Press

By the Pleasing Countenance of My Superiors

Thomas Cook, Esq. J.P. was one of many immigrants of middling income and status who early in their life threw in their lot with the young Colony of NSW. Like many, Thomas Cook made his contribution without achieving a major place in the history books or leaving behind enough of a record to present a complete picture of his life. Nevertheless, sufficient can be found to provide some fascinating glimpses of the man, the magistrate and of the village of Dungog in the mid-nineteenth century.

An good image of Thomas Cook as a magistrate can be built up from the chance survival of the Magistrates Letterbooks of the Dungog Court in which is preserved much of his official outward correspondence, particularity from 1837 throughout the 1840s, dealing with a wide range of issues.[1] From these letters Thomas Cook, Esq. appears an active and intelligent magistrate, though we also have an early complaint making the opposite claim, namely of 'the inactivity of the police force, under the orders of Mr. Cook'.[2] Cook makes suggestions regarding the training of new arrivals to minimize accidental death, he badgers the government in Sydney for funds to improve the facilities at Dungog, to pay arrears owed people employed under him, and to secure blankets for the local natives. Cook is prepared to argue with the local landowners over legalities and shows occasional sympathy to those convicts and ex-convicts, who come before him.[3] Not that this was enough to have made him loved by those outside the law, and in at least one case a bushranger named Opossum Jack is reported to have made threats against him.[4] Cook also made efforts to assist the local people who were rapidly being displaced by the new settlers, making efforts to secure sufficient blankets and also to intervene, even if ineffectually, in at least one case where an overseer was holding Aboriginal women against the wishes of their male kin.[5]

Thomas Cook (c.1788 – 1866), son of merchant Robert Cook, was born in Paisley, Scotland, (near Glasgow) arriving with his wife of eleven years and their four children in Sydney on the *Eldon* from Greenock (also near Glasgow) via Hobart Town in April 1834.[6] Cook was appointed a 'Magistrate of the Territory' on 5th November that year, becoming the Police Magistrate of Port Stephens.[7] Cook replaced a Captain Moffiat who had become involved in a dispute with the Australian Agricultural Company (AAC), which owned much of the land in the district and had even paid part of his salary. Cook's quick appointment, at an increased salary, may have been due to his connection (their wives were sisters), to Colonel Snodgrass, former commandant of the mounted police and member of the Legislative Council.[8] From Port Stephens Cook was 'directed to visit once a fortnight' the 'township of Dungog' where cattle stealing was seen as a major problem.[9] The Williams River district, on which Dungog lies, was soon after Thomas Cook's arrival the scene of much uproar with the deaths of five convict shepherds in what was at first thought was a general native uprising and about which it was reported that: 'Our various letters are loud in their complaints of the inactivity of the police magistrate Mr. Cooke, …'[10]

Soon after, in 1837 when the police districts were reorganised, Cook was appointed Police Magistrate of both Upper William and Port Stephens, but in a moved intended to distance the magistrate from the influence of the AAC, he was now to reside at Dungog.[11] Cook served as Police Magistrate at Dungog (travelling once a fortnight to the court at Stroud within Port Stephens) from 1837 until 1843. Thereafter he continued to reside at Dungog on his property

Auchentorlie (named after an estate at his native Paisley), acting as a local magistrate and also registrar and coroner. Sometime around 1860, Thomas Cook left Dungog for Woollahra in Sydney where he died in 1866 aged 78; his wife Mary survived him by a few years, also dying in Woollahra in 1871.[12]

Cook seems to have firmly believed in the authority that he represented and in its power and duty to control and help those who this authority deemed needed such control and assistance. When asked if a loan should be raised to encourage immigration to the colonies the answer of 'Thomas Cook, Esq., Police Magistrate, Dungog' was: 'I do think were such a scheme adopted, it would instantly operate in favour of the Colony, not only as regards its agricultural and commercial prosperity, but in its best interests, the moral improvement of the people.'[13] This interest in 'moral improvement' is perhaps what involved Thomas Cook in a sectarian controversy during the 1840s that first brings him to wider public notice.

In the early period of many settlements the court house was the first and for long the only public building. As such, court houses were often used on Sundays by the various Christian groups for services, and in the absence of an ordained minister or priest it was not unknown for a prominent member of the community to read services or simply from the bible. This Cook appears to have done as Police Magistrate, practicing a 'voluntary performance of Divine Worship' which in 1837 (when presumably Cook first commenced it), was praised by the Lord Bishop of Australia, who gave 'a set of church books'.[14]

However the degree of 'voluntary performance' involved when a magistrate requested his ticket-of-leave constables to attend services is questionable, and when the Irish Catholic background of some of these constables is combined with a Presbyterian Scots magistrate, the opportunities for conflict grow. Such a conflict appears to have become public in March 1840 when the editor of the *Australasian Chronicle* launched an attack on 'the most tyrannical, illegal, and arbitrary' of proceedings. This was the dismissal of the lock-up keeper and a constable at Dungog - both Catholics and one a veteran of 'the Peninsula' - for 'refusing to betray the faith' of their forefathers. This was an act of 'religious intolerance' that Cook compounded when he advertised for replacements with the notice that 'none but Protestants need apply'.[15] In the same issue as this editorial, the details of Cook's behaviour were given by a local witness, including his demand that all constables and ticket-of-leave men attend his Sunday service on pain of either dismissal or having their tickets revoked. It seems the lock-up keeper, James Boland, and ordinary constable, Patrick Coleman had refused to attend Cook's service after being talked to by a Catholic priest. The writer also complained that Cook had refused the use of the court house or the barracks to Catholics and their visiting priest, the Rev. E. Mahony. The same writer also claimed that Cook had been nearly dismissed the previous year due to complaints made and that none but those in fear of Cook attended his Sunday services.[16]

The following Sunday Cook appears to have defended his actions to those attending the service and blamed the interference of the priest concerned, the Rev. Mahony.[17] The controversy was taken up in other papers, with the very non-Catholic *Sydney Herald* agreeing in Cook's 'total unfitness for the magisterial office' but expressing the view that to attack him 'under the influence of sectarian feeling' rather than on 'public grounds' was not the best. The *Sydney Monitor* in quoting the *Sydney Herald* felt that this paper merely feared that Cook's Presbyterian zeal might overflow beyond Catholics to include 'Episcopalians'.[18]

The *Australasian Chronicle* followed up later in the month with the statement that Cook had received a letter from the Colonial Secretary about his 'protestant only' notice and had offered the two men their positions back but only on the promise that they would continue to attend his Sunday services. The editor asserted that they 'submitted' with 'want staring them in the face'. This editor went on to claim that Cook regularly used publicly paid officers to perform his private business and called for his dismissal.[19]

In early May 1840, Cook wrote to the *Sydney Herald* to defend himself. He began by denying that he had nearly been dismissed the previous year, claiming that in fact he was 'honored and gratified by the pleasing countenance' of his superiors. As to the Sunday services, they were well attended and often had a Rev. Mr. Ross from Paterson preaching at them. Cook however did not deny the charges of forcing people to attend his services, claiming that both the 'Roman Catholic Clergyman' and surprisingly the 'Clerk of the Bench', had encouraged his constables 'in the dereliction of duty for the sake of *their* religion'.[20] Presumably Cook meant a duty to attend his services. He added that the need for 'only Protestants' was 'necessary for the security and good order of the District' and denied ever refusing the use of the court house to the 'Roman Catholic Clergyman'.[21]

The *Australasian Chronicle* published a letter supporting its views on Cook by one who signed himself 'A Subscriber & A Protestant', while Cook's defence only led it to renew its calls for Cook's dismissal.[22] It also brought forth a short note from P. H. Magrane, the Dungog Clerk of the Bench, denying all accusations of interference on his part with the constables and also stating that Cook's letter contained other 'unfounded' statements, which Magrane refused to go into details about.[23] This notice of Magrane's was reprinted in the

Australasian Chronicle with the addition: 'Mr Magrane does not seem to be aware that "all things are lawful" to a certain description of "saints". – Ed.'[24] At the end of May 1840 two more letters were published from residents of Dungog, one denying the claims made by Cook in his *Sydney Herald* letter about the numbers attending his services and the near loss of his position, and another detailing Cook's refusal to hear any cases brought by Mr Hooke, a large landowner with whom Cook was at odds (over shooting a pig), which according to the writer resulted in Hooke's assigned servants not being punished.[25]

Throughout all this public controversy Thomas Cook as Police Magistrate was maintaining a regular correspondence with Sydney based officials, including the Colonial Secretary. This correspondence is preserved in the Dungog Magistrates Letterbooks and in his letters very few hints regarding the controversies he was involved in are given by Cook. An exception being the copy of a note to John Hooke:

> Police Office
>
> Dungog, 24th April, 1840.
>
> Sir,
> I do myself the honor to inform you that until you make an ample apology for the contempt shown to this Bench the last time you visited this Court House I must decline entertaining any cases you may be disposed to bring before me.
>
> I have the honor to be Sir
> your most obedient servant,
> Thomas Cook, JP
> Police Magistrate.
> To John Hooke Esq,
> Croom Park.[26]

The controversies continued with perhaps one helping to fuel another with Michael Ryan, who also wrote to the *Australasian Chronicle,* complaining that Cook had denied him a publican's license because he was a Catholic. Michael Ryan provided letters of recommendation from a number of local landowners (including Hooke) and claimed that Cook had told him he would grant him a license, on the strength of which a 'house' had been built.[27] Cook in writing to Ryan simply says his lack of letters of recommendation from Paterson, from where he came, and 'unpardonable reports' lead to his declining to grant a license.[28] A month after this, when Philip Magrane resigned as Clerk of the Bench in July, this was naturally ascribed by the *Australasian Chronicle* to Magrane's being Catholic and Cook a 'sectarian magistrate'.[29]

In August the *Australasian Chronicle* was on the attack again, this time overjoyed that 'some settlers from the Upper Williams' River' had come to Sydney to complain of Cook, and publishing two letters of Cook's thanking people for assisting him in various ways - the implication presumably being that these were forms of bribery.[30] Continuing the following month, the paper referred to an investigation and also published a letter in which Michael Ryan, the denied licensee, provoked Cook in his own court to declare him 'a d --- d rascal' - a shocking use of language at the time.[31] This was presumably at the time Michael Ryan was arrested for keeping a disorderly house, the same letter by Cook also revealing that Ryan, also known as 'Mickie the Priest' had been reported earlier as a receiver of stolen goods.[32]

Having carried on its anti-Cook campaign since March 1840 the controversy widened in scope when in October the 'Auxiliary Catholic Institute of Hunter's River' carried a series of motions drawing the attention of Magistrate Cook's activities to the Institute's Central Committee in Sydney, including his 'unmerited insults to the Catholics of the colony'. Attending the meeting and proposer of the first motion was Cook's former Clerk of the Bench, P. H. Magrane ('M'Grane').[33] This rather organisational and rhetorical move on the part of Catholics prompted the *Sydney Gazette* to begin beating the gong and issuing warnings of a Catholic takeover. According to the *Sydney Gazette* the true object of 'Papists' and of this development of an 'Inquisition' to put officials on trial, was now evident; a plague was beginning, but these people the *Gazette* dismisses as 'petty shopkeepers' who are liable to use aliases. The editor defended Cook, who it declared had reason to believe a priest had 'interfered with a policeman'. No direct mention was made of the compulsion to attend Sunday services but instead an ingenious argument was made that Cook was saving the consciences of Catholics from the clash of needing to serve a Protestant authority. After all, no one could trust an 'ignorant Papist, where a Priest interferes'. The editorial then moved onto an even higher level of hysteria, declaring that the Catholic Institute has 'treason for its aim, and blood for its end' and finished with a call for Protestants to unite.[34]

Having reached this frenzied pitch the Cook sectarian controversy seems to have gradually petered out. The *Australasian Chronicle* did continue to publish complaints against Police Magistrate Cook, such as another letter from a Dungog resident going over some of the old issues and adding one of cowardice in pursuit, or lack of pursuit, of local bushrangers. The writer added that this anti-Catholic magistrate had happily directed armed Catholic ticket-of-leave men guard his family during the incursion and called again for an investigation.[35] Another wrote the following year detailing how Cook had casually ordered twenty lashes and did not care when fifty were administered instead.[36]

But just as Cook's problems with Catholics appeared to be fading he managed to annoy the Protestants of Dungog. It seems that on Sunday, December 26th 1840 Cook began reading a sermon from a printed book of such sermons, as he had often done. The difference this time being that an ordained 'Presbyterian clergyman', the Rev. Mr. Comrie was present. There is some uncertainty whether Mr Comrie was late arriving or was in fact present when Cook began preaching. In either case Cook continued to read, while signalling Mr. Comrie to sit.[37] The end result of this behaviour was a meeting of Presbyterians at Stephenson's Inn, Dungog a few months later at which it was agreed not to attend services at the court house but instead to use an unoccupied house offered by a community member. A writer to the *Sydney Herald* recounted Cook questioning the Rev. Mr. Comrie publicly as to his intentions when told this decision and that Cook subsequently put up a notice declaring that prayer meetings would no longer be held at the court house but that musters of constables would continue.[38]

Despite this seeming unpopularity, Thomas Cook was to remain acting as a magistrate in Dungog for many years. Cook's difficulties, if that is what he felt them to be, may have reached their peak in 1841. Nothing either good or bad is heard of him in 1842, and although in early 1843 a fire is thought to have been deliberately lit on his property, that same year it was proposed to collect subscriptions 'to purchase a piece of plate' to present to the 'late Police Magistrate' in appreciation of his services.[39]

The collection was because Cook ceased acting as a paid Police Magistrate in early 1843. While such a token of appreciation may not be all it seems (this was a meeting to discuss a meeting to collect money), the loss of his position as a Police Magistrate does not appear to have been directly due to any previous complaints. Rather it was likely due to a gradual reduction in paid Police Magistrates throughout NSW and their replacement with local landowner's who were Justice's of the Peace performing the duty unpaid.[40] It is probable that this was part of a gradual reduction in Police Magistrates taking place whenever it was considered 'there are a sufficient number of unpaid Magistrates to do the duty'.[41] Cook would have lost his position by 1844 in any case, as by then the government had reverted to nearly all unpaid magistrates as a cost saving measure.[42] Cook continued to be a Justice of the Peace and acted therefore as one of these unpaid magistrates, though for a time local lobbying did attempt to have the paid position restored.[43]

In 1845, when after some lobbying it seemed certain that the paid Police Magistrate's position would not be restored, a collection was made and a 'purse' of £43 was presented to Cook in appreciation of his services with notice of this reprinted a number of times.[44] However this public expression of appreciation brought out at least one enemy of Cook's who roundly condemned the whole exercise as a farce and published details of the collection of the £43 showing that some £30 of it came from staff of the AAC, and that money from Dungog was only donated by various workers within the legal establishment and ticket-of-leave holders, with nothing at all from 'Landed proprietors' or 'Gentlemen'.[45] The implication was that Cook put pressure on those he could and that he was in favour with the AAC but not with the respectable folk of Dungog itself.

Having ceased to be paid as a Police Magistrate, Cook did not cease acting as a Dungog magistrate since he was still a Justice of the Peace. Cook and his family had settled on the Williams River and at some point it seems purchased land that had been part of Crawford Logan Brown's 1829 Cairnsmore grant just north of Dungog village, which he named Auchentorlie.[46] And in 1839, Cook also bought eight perches of town blocks for a cost of nearly £50 within the area of the recently laid out village of Dungog, presumably for purposes of speculation; all but a handful of these allotments were sold and Cook was the largest single purchaser.[47]

In addition to general duties as a magistrate, Cook also acted as Commissioner for Affidavits, Coroner, Commissioner of Crown lands, and could order out the mounted troopers when occasion demanded.[48] Recognised as the 'senior magistrate', Cook often had a role in community positions, such as the convening and chairing of meetings; including one meeting concerning roads in which his opening address was described as 'a most eloquent and appropriate speech'.[49] In May 1849, Cook was appointed to the new District Council of 'Raymond Terrace and Dungog and again in 1853.[50] It is in 1851 that Cook received another address in appreciation of his services, one reputedly signed by nearly 500 'respectable persons'.[51] Also in 1851 his name headed a petition from the residents of Dungog requesting road repairs, and in 1854 he was part of a group that examined the children at the new National School and provided the speech in reply.[52]

The newspapers that are the source of most of our knowledge about Thomas Cook focus much on his official activities, but occasionally more personal aspects slip through, as when in October 1845 Cook lost his watch on a farm on the Williams River. He advertised a £2 reward for the return of this 'plain gold watch' with the inscription God and King in French.[53] Later, in early 1848, Cook nearly drowned when he slipped fording a flooded river near his home; he managed to grab hold of a tree trunk to pull himself out, while a passersby rescued his horse.[54] At the end of this same year a severe storm damaged the roof of his house at Auchentorlie.[55] The following year he advertised some 40 acres of farm land to let, land Cook claims yielded 35 to 40 bushels of wheat per acre and situated where 'pilfering (the greatest curse to the small settler) is unknown'.[56] And a few years later it would seem all controversy of the past was forgotten as the 'senior magistrate of the district' and his daughter 'Miss Cook' opened with a bottle of sherry 'The Union Bridge' over Verge Creek midway between Dungog and Clarence Town.[57]

Apart from their names little is know about Cook's family either in Dungog or Scotland. He left an 'only sister' Sarah in Scotland, who died in 1836.[58] We also know that Thomas Cook was unlucky with his children, with two dying in early adulthood while living at Dungog, Henrietta, his eldest daughter aged 20 'after a short illness' in 1842, and his youngest son Thomas in 1852 aged 24 from an infection after being bled by a 'quack doctoress' using an 'unclean lancet' according to the local newspaper.[59] Cook's eldest son Robert did not outlive him very long, dying in London in 1874, while nothing is known of the remaining daughter who helped him open the Union Bridge, Janet.[60]

In 1855, Cook is naturally part of the notables involved in a local patriotic fund formed to support Britain's just commenced war with Russia.[61] In that same year, and ready as usual to make a speech, Cook lay the foundation stone of the 'Established Church of Scotland'.[62] However, this last seemingly innocent participation in a community event may hint at deeper divisions within the community, for less than a month afterwards another laying of a foundation stone for a Presbyterian Church occurred in Dungog. On this occasion local landowner George Mackay lay the foundation stone for the Presbyterian Church of Eastern Australia, associated with the Free Church of Scotland.[63]

It is unclear if this religious division within the Presbyterian community was a cause or effect of other divisions within Dungog, or indeed even if it was a significant division. But a reported speech of Cook's and a further public controversy is suggestive of factions, and religion was a significant 'grouping' factor in people's lives at that time. Cook for example appears to have been aware that his career in Dungog had not been the smoothest, being reported in a speech of appreciation of one of Dungog's doctors to have said: 'He had been a magistrate in the neighbourhood for many years, and though he had trod on the toes of many, still he felt that, having done his duty, he had nothing to fear ...'[64]

While this speech of Cook claims that he did what he considered right without fear or favour, another incident around this time raises some doubts. In this controversy, Cook, though not a major participant, is not seen in a good light. The issue concerned the dismissal of the long time Chief Constable of Dungog, seemingly for his having come into conflict with a drunken J.P. In 1854 Thomas Abbott had charged Mr. Foster, J.P. with being drunk and disorderly. Soon after this he was accused by Foster of using insulting language to a magistrate. In both cases the presiding magistrates preferred to send the case off to the Attorney-General rather than face either dismissing their Chief Constable or fellow Magistrate.[65] Soon after Abbott was ordered to live within the town, while Abbott claimed that his house was only one quarter of a mile from the Court House.[66] Despite his arguments, Thomas Abbott was dismissed as Chief Constable for failing to reside in the town. At this time the magistrates were Chas. H. Green, John Hooke, George Mackay, Thomas Cook and Thomas Holmes.[67] The case is unclear (except for the obvious nearness of Abbott's still standing house to the town and where he had lived throughout most of his tenure as Chief Constable), but Cook and the other magistrates appear to have participated, even if only by omission, in the victimisation of the less powerful for the purposes of revenge and the dismissal of a man unwilling to turn a blind eye.

Despite this unpleasantness a similar subscription in appreciation of Cook's services at Dungog to that of 1845 was made in 1857, marking twenty years of such service. A sum of £34.2s was gathered, with this time the AAC uninvolved and, although some prominent storekeepers are, none of the major landowners' names appear in the published list this time either.[68] This testimonial notice is also reprinted a number of times in the *Sydney Morning Herald*.[69] The following year Cook received another testimonial, for £100 with an attached subscription list, and again, although two of his fellow magistrates, Dowling and Foster, are listed, the others are not, nor are the names of such prominent local landowners as Alison, Hooke or Mackay.[70]

Seemingly ever willing to take on any court related job, Cook in 1858 becomes the Dungog 'Registrar of Births, Deaths and Marriages'.[71] However the long period of quite for Cook, at least as far as the newspapers are concerned, ended in this same year. In that year the Ross family was drowned during a flood and their deaths investigated. A jury found that not enough had been done to assist the family and this resulted in an angry exchange of letters in the *Maitland Mercury* as various parties sought to justify their actions. As a result, Thomas Cook was much abused in a letter written by James Newell who hinted at factions within the community.[72]

By this time Cook was probably in his late 50s or perhaps early 60s and perhaps spent less of his time sitting on the bench than breeding horses, for in May 1859 he is selling 12 horses by auction at West Maitland.[73] Not much is heard of Thomas Cook in the next few years, though in early 1863 he is still listed as a J.P. at Dungog.[74] Then suddenly Cook is making a petition to the NSW Legislative Assembly, 'complaining of unjust deprivation of his salary as a police magistrate.'[75]

The loss of his position as Justice of the Peace by Cook may have been part of a general government reform whereby numerous names were removed from the list of Justices of the Peace for a variety of reasons.[76] However, Cook first presents his petition in July 1863, prior to the announcement of the government reforms and again in April 1865, 'complaining of having been dismissed without compensation'. This matter is still unresolved on the death of Thomas Cook in February 1866 at Woollahra, Sydney.[77] The decline of the status of Cook seems complete when in 1870 a petition is presented to the NSW Legislative Assembly 'from Mrs Mary Cook, widow of the late Mr. Thomas Cook, who was for many years Police Magistrate at Port Stephens, praying that the services of her late husband might be taken into consideration'.[78] Mary died the following year.[79]

This rather modest end to the career of Thomas Cook is not the final word however. Dogged by controversy throughout his life it seems to have followed him long afterwards. This occurs in the form of newspaper accounts in the following century declaring him to have been a flogging magistrate and linking him with a number of exciting tales of death, convict murder and avenging bushrangers. These sensational stories find no trace in the newspapers of the day and are perhaps variations on a single story and may even relate to another

Cook entirely.[80] They appear to have originated in the work of 'The Man in the Mask', the pen name of a number of contributors to *Smith's Weekly*, one of whom was undoubtedly Gordon Bennett, Dungog born and son of the founder of the *Dungog Chronicle*.[81] Bennett also wrote other inaccurate pieces in which Thomas Cook is usually referred to as Captain Cook. This is a title Cook seems never to have used himself, although at the time of the sectarian controversy he was accused of doing so by at least one writer.[82]

Thomas Cook, father, Presbyterian, magistrate, J.P., letter writer, horse breeder, landowner, opener of bridges, speech-maker, and at times a figure of some controversy. Despite this list, our picture of the man remains incomplete and the temptation to fill in the gaps in the manner of Gordon Bennett is great, though in modern times we might emphasise his family relations and political interactions over the number of floggings meted out or murderous convicts encountered. For the time being, until further information is uncovered, we must be content with what tantalising glimpses the often sketchy historical record has left us.

FUNERAL.—The Friends of the late THOMAS COOK, Esq., deceased, are respectfully invited to attend his Funeral; to move from his late residence, corner of Denison-street and Point Piper Road, THIS (Monday) MORNING, at half-past 9 o'clock precisely. JOHN HILL and SON, Undertakers, William and Riley streets.

This research on Thomas Cook is ongoing and this work will be revised accordingly from time to time. If any reader has any information about Thomas Cook please write to the author at – ChideStudyPress@gmail.com

Magistrates' Letterbook for the police districts of Dungog and Port Stephens, New South Wales, 1834-1839.

(Manuscript, National Library of Australia.)

This anomalous community

Dungog Magistrates' Letterbook, 1834-1839.[83]

Bound in a single volume of copied letters, running from the beginning of 1834 until early 1839, is a record of the outward correspondence of magistrates sitting at the newly established courthouse at what was first referred to as 'Upper William' and from about August 1834, Dungog.[84] This correspondence was to local landowners, magistrates of surrounding districts, the Commissioner of the nearby Australian Agricultural Company (AAC), and of course to numerous functionaries in Sydney including the Superintendent of Convicts, the Colonial Storekeeper and most often, the Colonial Secretary.

This outward correspondence by Dungog's magistrates contains numerous insights into local administration in the convict period of Australian history, capturing as it does a slice of life across a wide range of matters over a few years in the late 1830s. The Letterbook gives a glimpse into Australian history at a time when convicts, indigenous people and newly granted landowners lived side by side on the edge of white settlement, some 150 miles and at least two hard days travel from Sydney. Perhaps most suggestive of the basis of this 'anomalous community' is the paradoxical phrase - 'free by servitude' – frequently used to refer to those members of it no longer in formal custody.

The range of matters dealt with in the letters is broad; from the punishment of prisoners and routine ticket-of-leave applications, to collecting statistical information, forwarding on of fines, fees and 'Benevolent Society' collections, as well as the ordering of supplies and hiring of constables, including 'scourgers'. The importance of the postal system is underlined, even if only through the many complaints made about its slowness. While in the payment of rewards or improvements to buildings, the slowness of the colonial administration itself is seen. Much is also revealed about this society through the nature of the most common offenses mentioned, absconding, being absent from ones district of ticket, cattle stealing, and the harbouring of absconders. Also exposed in the letters is this administration's weakness in dealing with the oppression of the original inhabitants of the Williams River valley by those nominally under its authority.[85]

Administrative methods are also clearly seen, such as the practice of referring to a convict or prisoners in general terms in a letter and then adding the name in the margin. Identification of convicts was through their ship of arrival, and sometimes length of sentence; a system that seems to have worked, with only one case where identification could not be determined.[86] Other nuances of the administration's procedures can be drawn from the material of the Letterbook itself; the varying handwriting as the scribe or Clerk of the Bench changes, or in the red sealing wax used to glue in the occasional loose sheet. Another touch, this time of the hierarchy inherent to the administration, is seen in the formal acknowledgments graded according to the status of the person addressed, as in: 'Sir,' 'I remain,' 'I have the honour…,' and 'I do myself the honour ...'[87]

The role of the Magistrate in balancing the legal requirements of a convict based system with landowner's requirements for labour is seen in letters that discuss punishments that lessen the usefulness of an assigned convict.[88] A role observed clearly in a dispute between landowners over the transfer of a convict with the sale of land.[89] While the checking of identification for possible absconders is an issue displayed in the Magistrate's frustration that this was not being done enough.[90] This inbuilt tension within the system is seen to increase when the landowner is the Australian Agricultural Company, an ongoing source of concern for a magistrate given charge of the AAC's area and it seems purposely stationed outside it.[91]

Aspects of the lives of those on the edge of this society are glimpsed in cases where a convict is certified mad, a mother is sent to gaol because destitute, and an original inhabitant speaks English sufficiently to tell the Magistrate that women of his group are being held against his (and presumably their) will.[92] Names appear and then disappear back into the obscurity of the past. Official letters though these are, some of the personality of Police Magistrate Thomas Cook also slips through from time to time. In his concern for the accidental deaths of young newly arrived convicts and his suggestions for improved training, his frustration with the actions of the AAC, and his efforts with the original inhabitants. Cook's seeming callousness over the death of a servant, and in his assumption of faking by a sick prisoner draw a picture that is well within the range of average human strengths and frailties.[93]

The control and punishment of the convict population of the district was a major function of a magistrate and in fact, the first letter in the Letterbook complains that two years on a road gang is inadequate power to punish absconders.[94] This was written by the first magistrate of Upper Williams to use the Letterbook, George Mackenzie, J.P., who at the end of January 1834 was investigating the activities of William O'Neil, 'here by servitude,' who was occupying Crown land on the Clarence Town road and having no visible means of sustenance was suspected of receiving and stealing cattle. Having been convicted of harbouring prisoners of the Crown he is given notice to quit.[95] R. G. Moffat (Captain 17th Regiment) adds the following March that O'Neil is 'a most notorious Sly Grog seller'.[96]

In addition to convicts, fear of the original inhabitants was also great. In April this same first year of the Letterbook, a request for arms and ammunition was made because 'at present the Aborigines are very troublesome,' with mounted police from Patrick's Plains also requested due to a spearing and 'well grounded alarm'.[97] In the same month a John Flinn was killed in the camp of 'our own tribe,' 'and although Blacks may not be considered as being of such importance as Whites in these cases,' Moffatt nevertheless committed the accused murderer for trial.[98]

Some of the early letters are signed not by magistrates but by the Clerk of the Bench, D. F. MacKay, a local landowner. MacKay wrote to nearby Paterson for assistance in July 1835 when he felt 'the Blacks have again commenced committing serious depredations in the neighborhood,' including spearing cattle in the bush opposite his own residence.[99] Earlier in the year, a reward was offered for 'an Aboriginal Black named Jemmy' for 'many outrages'.[100] While the following year reference was made to the murder of Mackenzie's men on the Gloucester in May 1835, accused were Jemmi and Kotra Jacki.[101] Lawrence Myles, J.P., also requested mounted police in May 1836 under the shadow of this attack, citing 'intelligence that the Blacks are becoming more troublesome'.[102]

Dealing legally with the local Aboriginal people meant talking to them and in July 1834, a request was made for the Rev Threlkeld, a missionary working on the nearby coast who had learned a related Aboriginal language, to act as interpreter in King vs. Jacky.[103] Possibly, this was the same Jacky sent down to Maitland the year after for the 1831 spearing of a Robert Weddis, from which he would go by steamer to Sydney.[104]

The constables used by these magistrates for escorting prisoners such as Jacky were usually ex-convicts and often cause difficulties themselves. In September 1834, Senior Constable Thomas Rodwell was replaced in his position due to being intoxicated 'while in the discharge of his duty'. His replacement was Michael Connolly, a ticket-of-leave man and former constable at Bathurst.[105] A few years later, a constable brought in his prisoners drunk, having given them rum at a Public House near Paterson – 'the day being wet & cold'. Magistrate Cook seems to have sympathized and waived the charge of neglect but did fine the Senior Constable £5 for breach of the Licensing Act; half of this to go as a reward to the informer, in this case the Police Magistrate at Paterson.[106]

However, when a constable was found to be reliable, Thomas Cook at least was prepared to act accordingly. In February 1839 for example, Cook recommended that Robert Mason replace James Edwards as constable at Stroud, this was despite Mason having been dismissed by Major Sullivan; though 'for no removable act' in Cook's opinion. Mason was sent to Stroud that same day with a note to the AAC requesting he be provided with provisions and accommodation 'on usual terms'.[107] Cook was very pleased with the work of what seems to have been a lone constable placed at Gloucester, Patrick Conway, who gave 'good service in taking bushrangers and putting down sly grog shops'. Cook felt that his 1s per day pay should be increased.[108]

Around 1834, there was difficultly getting people to act as a magistrate. George Mackenzie's property, for example, was 16 miles from the courthouse at Dungog, which was 'directly in the through fare between the AAC's extensive establishment and Hunter River.'[109] The AAC's property between Port Stephens and Gloucester to the east of Dungog meant many convicts needed to be dealt with, while it was on the Hunter River that settlers and police were to be found. However, having a magistrate on this privately owned estate carried its own issues. Consequently in 1837, Thomas Cook, originally appointed as paid Police Magistrate at Port Stephens (as opposed to the local landowning Justices of the Peace acting as unpaid magistrates), was appointed to Dungog (or Upper Williams) but with responsibility for Port Stephens and its court at Stroud also.[110]

It is for this reason that the bulk of the correspondence in the Letterbook occurs from 1837 under the name of Thomas Cook after he has taken up residence at Dungog rather than simply visiting from Stroud and runs until early 1839 when the volume becomes full.[111] But having Cook as a paid magistrate did not entirely solve the shortage of magistrates as in many cases, such as the assignment of convicts, two magistrates were needed. This need to get a second magistrate was a constant concern, with Cook explaining four years into his appointment that it was easier to get Johnston from Paterson than Esbworth from Port Stephens as he lived at Booral, which was 30 miles from Stroud.[112] This delay in getting the required second magistrate often led Cook to send prisoners on to Sydney rather than wait.[113]

Cook's first letter in the Letterbook is one of many administrative ones, a routine passing on of a ticket-of-leave application and the answering of a circular requesting information about facilities within his district, namely that Singleton's Mill is the only public flour mill, located 2 miles above Clarence Town.[114] However, not all is routine and in May 1835, Cook gives a detailed report on the escape from Dungog lock-up of Timothy Fogarty, a captured bushranger who managed to lever down the wood paneling of his cell, remove the outer bricks and then scramble over the 10 foot yard wall. Although a constable was living inside the courthouse, and the jailer and his family also lived in a small room off the court house, Cook states that 'from sundown to sunrise' there was no observation of prisoners.[115] Other escapees passed through the area, with one from Port Macquarie described as wearing a green cloth jacket, blue trousers, blue waistcoat, check or stripped pants and a straw hat.[116]

Cook also had to deal with those who had lived in the valley of the Williams River before convicts and their land granted masters appeared. In the beginning of 1836, for example, he is fearful of a rescue attempt being made on 'Black' prisoners being sent to Newcastle and requested two troopers from Maitland.[117] This was granted and in September, MacKay, as Clerk of the Bench, wrote that 'Jimmy' was sent under escort of two mounted police and a reward of £10 was to be paid.[118]

The newly established settlement of Upper Williams, soon known as Dungog, was a convenient link between the AAC lands to the east and the much larger settlement at Maitland on the Hunter River, and this position was a reason for its early courthouse. However, Dungog was not so convenient for those living along the Allyn River, which runs parallel to the Williams, and settlers there wrote in 1836 to request they be allowed to deal through magistrates at Paterson rather than Dungog.[119] The question of whether Allyn River settlers belonged to Paterson or Dungog was part of the evolving administrative organisation of the Sydney based government and as part of this, a census was to be taken, which in turn required the district's boundaries be defined. In 1836 these were, from Singleton's Mill, the head of navigation above Clarence Town, then west to Stony Creek, that creek being the south-west boundary, then north to the head of the Williams, including Wallarobba.[120]

As well as assisting in matters of overall colonial administration, the Magistrate spent much time dealing with the relations between convicts and the masters to whom they were assigned. As such, Thomas Cook was part of a government bureaucracy that included the 'Board of Assignment of Servants,' responsible for where convicts were placed and to which Cook as Magistrate could only make recommendations if a crime were not involved. In October 1836, Cook was investigating a complaint of J. Devlin, assigned to Mr Holmes; Devlin is described as 'a poor simpleton'.[121] Later that same year, James Williams is requesting 'slop Clothing'.[122] The following year, Joseph Webster found himself removed from service with Mr Rogers for complaining from 'Peak, and not ill usage'. Cook felt Webster was 'one of those Convicts who pretend to know Rules Laws, and regulations better than their superiors,' and feared this 'leveling Spirit Contaminate whatever they come near.' Cook suggested Webster go to the 'Ironed Gang' at Port Macquarie.[123] The assignment of servants did not always work out, as when Cook ordered that Sarah Robinson be removed from the house of Michael Doyle – 'She being a greater burden than a comfort to an industrious Family'.[124]

Thomas Cook was an active magistrate and often wrote in an attempt to improve facilities, such as the lock-up at Dungog.[125] He was also responsible for the facilities at Stroud, but here he needed to rely on the Australian Agricultural Company, a bureaucracy it seems every bit as slow as the government's, and so he also wrote to speed up the new lock-up at Stroud.[126] As well as facilities, Cook frequently sent reminders about arrears of pay for his Lockup Keeper, John McGibbon, and about expenses paid during the 1837 Census.[127] Money was still owed McGibbon six months later and eight months after the census.[128] The system was not only slow but brutal, illustrated by Cook's request for 'scourging Cats' at the same time that he required ammunition, flints, and handcuffs; obtaining each from a different department of government.[129] In December 1837, a request was made for less violent but urgently needed 'fine foolscap paper and Quills'. Cook asked that these to be sent by the sloop *Northumberland* to Clarence Town, or if that has sailed, by steamer to Raymond Terrace.[130]

By 1837 relations with the first inhabitants appear to have improved with Cook exercising some discretion when he wrote that he felt it advisable to ignore the recently arrived McAuthy, despite a reward being posted for this Aboriginal man with the Scottish name. The Magistrate felt that the removal of two other Aboriginal people, named Calkie and Cobawn Paddy (presumably by arrest), had had an 'effect'.[131]

An aspect of relations with the original inhabitants of the Williams river valley and surrounding district was the annual blanket distribution, begun originally by Governor Macquarie. In March 1837, Cook requested such blankets, describing them as a 'comfort of the naked, houseless Blacks' 'during the inclemency of winter'.[132] Cook, as with his quills, describes the best route such blankets can reach him; first to Greenhills [Morpeth], then 'by Mr Cory's boat to the Paterson,' then by 'dry dray to Dungog'.[133] Lawrence Myles of Dungog evidently carried the blankets from Maitland instead and was still unpaid in October that year.[134] The return for blankets of 1837 shows 80 were distributed, including 20 from Stroud, with the comment that 'twenty more could have been bestowed'.[135] In the following two years, Cook wrote to William Barrow the Colonial Storekeeper to request 200 blankets to Clarence Town via the *Northumberland* or the AAC schooner *Carrington*.[136]

The return on 'Natives' taken at the blanket distribution for 1838 describes how only those 'most worthy of the boon' were selected, and that in general 'the conduct of all the Blacks in this neighbourhood has been quiet and praiseworthy during the last two years'. This Cook feels to be due to the amended Licensing Act, Oct 1835, which had effected a good reform on 'all classes of this anomalous community'.[137]

The anomalousness of the community is emphasised by the fact that, according to Cook, 'no convict can legally possess any money'. Cook goes on to say that it was usual for constables to search prisoners for the purpose of taking their money.[138] Presumably, Cook means to turn it over to the authorities. The month following this Cook does forward £2/9/- taken from a prisoner, which was 'the mode followed by me when any money was found in the pocket of convicts sent up for trial, it being illegal and unsafe for them to possess any means'. The money was to be put in the bank on their behalf. If this was not done, Cook feared the prisoner population would soon be too much.[139]

While Cook seems to have a mildly sympathetic view of the original inhabitants of his district, his attitude to those brought to Dungog by force does not show a similar one. With William Pepper, who had been a prevaricating witness in Cook's opinion and 'attempting to defeat the ends of justice,' Cook recommended the loss of his ticket.[140] In August 1837, James Lyman and John Cane also have their tickets withdrawn, the first for harboring a prisoner and attempting to bribe a constable, and the latter for stealing a jacket.[141] However, a magistrate's decisions were subject to review, and in July 1837 Cook's sentence of two years in the 'Ironed Gang' for James Howatt for slandering a Dr Whitfield was overturned by the Governor.[142]

Deaths, including accidental ones, were also the preserve of local magistrates and accidental death was not uncommon. At ‘Cairnsmore,’ the estate of Crawford Logan Brown, according to the deposition taken by Cook, William Mitten was ‘killed by an explosion of gunpowder which he himself had placed in a well for the purpose of blowing up the rock’.[143] That same month an inquest was held into the death of a servant of W. J. Forster, named William Wilson, killed by a falling tree.[144] Two months later there was another death by falling tree, this time on AAC property, of Robert Launders, who had just come to the colony. Cook was moved to think in terms of prevention and wrote to fellow Magistrate and sometime Commissioner of the AAC, Edward Ebsworth that, as this was one of four such cases in four months and that as many such accidents were due to ‘inexperienced youth,’ such people should be paired with ‘old hands’ to provide training.[145] It is not known if this was done. Cook was also concerned with drinking and the following year suggested a ban on selling more than 2 gallons at a time.[146]

In the administration of the law of his area, Cook required a close relationship with the AAC. Cook was Magistrate of two police districts, the Upper Williams River (courthouse, Dungog) and Port Stephens (courthouse, Stroud). The AAC, whose many convict shepherds caused much work for the court, was required to share some of the expenses, such as a new lock-up and payment of constables.[147] In 1837, the force Cook controlled within the Port Stephens district was three constables paid by the government and four constables plus a ‘scourger’ paid for by the AAC.[148]

The full force of the law under Police Magistrate Cook is laid out in the:

‘Statement of the Police force authorized and existing in the Districts of Port Stephens and Upper Williams River up to the 30th June 1837, viz:

Dungog	**Port Stephens**
1 Resident Magistrate	
1 Clerk	3 Ordinary Constables in Government Pay
1 Gaoler	a Clerk
1 District Constable	4 Ordinary Constables (one acting as Lockup keeper)
3 Ordinary Constables and 1 Scourger’[149]	and Scourger in AAC pay

The previous Chief Constable had been paid £75 per year and the current District Constable @ 3/- ‘per diem’.[150]

The Magistrate and his Clerk needed to make the trip once a fortnight from Dungog to Stroud to hear cases there and in October 1837 Cook wrote that he was too ill to make the trip ‘over the mountains’.[151] That Cook was a paid official of government rather than a local volunteer landowner is apparent when ill health delayed him in Sydney and he supplied a doctor’s certificate to back up this claim.[152]

In 1838, Cook gave a clear account of the budget of his domain in an estimate of expenses for the following year, including ‘absolutely necessary’ expenditure on facilities.[153]

Estimated Expense 1839

Dungog	
Magistrate	£250
Clerk	£100
Chief Constable	£75
Lock up Keeper	£54
3 Ordinary Constables	£139/10
Scourger	£40/10
	Total – £659

Port Stephens	
Lock up Keeper	£54
2 Ordinary Constables	£81
Scourger	£40/10
	Total - £175/10

Rations for Lockup & gaol	£40
Lighting	£2
Escort expenses	£3
Postages	£3
	Total – £48

Supplementary
Verandah for Courthouse "absolutely necessary"
£10
Rebuilt chimney
£4
Magistrates Rm (renovation)
£6
Minor repairs Court Hse/Lockup
£6
Lockup House with 2 strong rooms
£40

Total – £66

This came to an annual budget to run two police districts of £948 and 10 shillings.

Relations with the AAC were sometimes difficult, as with a dispute in August 1837 over the cost of feeding a prisoner in custody. According to Cook, 'when convicts are sent by their masters to any lock-up in the country, to await the appointed day for the coming of a Magistrate, it is understood the culprit brings his rations with him; but having once been before the Court and remanded, all subsequent expense falls on Government'.[154] This is a fine distinction about one's status in custody that must have left many convicts wondering where their next meal was coming from.

Sometime later Cook's frustrations in his dealings with the AAC is evident in the mild scorn he allows himself in a letter to fellow Magistrate Major Johnston, when he writes that the Commissioner of the AAC has discovered that he is 'on an equal footing with other respectable settlers in regard to the assignment regulations'.[155] Difficulties with the AAC over petty matters continued, however, such as when Cook wrote concerning a dispute between Thomas Brown, one of his constables based in Port Stephens and described by Cook as 'ready, steady and active in the performance of his duty,' and the AAC who had refused to sell the constable provisions from the public stores.[156] It was the government, Cook reminded the AAC, who had requested a lock-up keeper, two ordinary constables and a scourger be placed 'on the north side of the Williams'.

Cook is responsible for changes in personnel and must inform the Colonial Secretary that Alexander Hamilton, the lock-up keeper in Stroud is relieving for McGibbon in Dungog.[157] Also that John Powers has been appointed scourger at Stroud at 2s/3d per day and 'performs his duty well'.[158] Similar information was conveyed to Dumaresq at the AAC when it was recommended that John Powers continue as scourger and the AAC Commissioner reminded that this was not a claim on the AAC. In the same letter, Cook reported he would be visiting the next Tuesday and 'will be glad to listen to any case you or Mr Arkins may have to bring forward'.[159] Later in the year, McGibbon transferred to Stroud as lock-up keeper and was replaced in Dungog by James Boland.[160] In March 1838, Constable Brown resigned, eventually becoming a clerk in Sydney gaol.[161]

Some time during 1837, Cook's control over the AAC constables seems to have been withdrawn.[162] Nevertheless, Cook continued to complain about this large landowning company, this time to a fellow Police Magistrate, about being forced to hold court in a 'Common School Room'.[163] Perhaps the Colonial Secretary was also becoming frustrated with the complaints, however, in true bureaucratic style this official merely wrote to 'call your attention to the expediency of acting in concert with the Commissioner'.[164]

Due to the increasing number of absconders from the AAC, a 'small force of mounted police' commanded by Sir Rich Bourke KGB was established at Dungog at around the time Thomas Cook was established there. However, as Cook pointed out, no accommodation was available, but a 'slab-building' could be put up by Government party and a long requested Watch House and Lock-up keeper's apartments at the same time. All of which was 'now undisputedly necessary'.[165] In support of his feeling that more buildings and accommodation were needed, Cook provided the Colonial Secretary with a detailed description of what existed at the time in terms of Police buildings in Dungog. There was the Courthouse itself, off which was a small consulting room and 'a dark place' for securing property in charge of the Police.

The dimensions of the rooms were:

Court Room	18 feet by 14 feet with a 9 foot ceiling
Consulting Room	9 feet by 8 feet with a 9 foot ceiling
Place for books	9 feet by 6 feet with a 9 foot ceiling
Yard	80 feet by 54 feet and a 10 foot fence
Cells	7 feet by 4 feet, height 7½ feet[166]

The cells at the back of the Courthouse were surrounded by a high slab fence. It seems these cells were for prisoners sentenced to solitary confinement, although as Cook pointed out, they were not much good for this purpose as the prisoners could talk to each other. In these cells sometimes 8-10 prisoners could be kept for days or weeks awaiting a second magistrate. This was a 'great inconvenience,' though whether for Cook or the crowded prisoners is not clear.[167]

At least one prisoner complained enough to receive some attention from Cook, who wrote to Doctor Park at Paterson that he was sending Thomas Ford who had been sometime in the lock-up and wished to consult a medical practitioner for an 'imaginary disease'. Cook sent him to the Paterson lock-up where Dr Park could advise him.[168] A little later Cook seems to have modified his opinion, writing that Ford, who had been charged with cattle stealing, 'seems to labor under some nervous affliction – arising I believe from confinement and anxiety of mind'. Cook suggested Ford 'be either committed for trial or at once discharged'.[169]

The Magistrate often needed to deal with problems relating to the mental state of convicts. In November the same year Ford's 'anxiety of mind' was recognised, another prisoner, this time in the Watch house at Stroud, attempted to commit suicide. John Williams was declared insane and sent to Newcastle.[170] Early in 1839 a servant of James Walker of Brookfield was declared not fit for service due to his being subject to 'common fits'. Walker was therefore short of hands.[171] Other cases seem less clear, as when the wife of local landowner Mr Hooke requested leniency for a Mary Williams, who had been absent without leave and placed in solitary confinement. Later Mary was declared 'filthy' and diseased and sent to Newcastle.[172] And in another case, the situation was clearer but the solution less so when Cook, concerning a Mrs Park, wrote: 'what is best to be done for a woman in her destitute situation'? All he could do was send her and her two children to Newcastle gaol 'to await His Excellency's pleasure regarding them'.[173]

In addition to legal matters, the postal service was also part of a magistrate's responsibilities and in the Letterbook's opposite end are a few letters written concerning post office matters. This was because at first the Clerk of the Bench, Duncan MacKay, also handled postal matters. The first of these letters is in fact MacKay's resignation in which he states that William Cormack would act as Post Officer but not if he gets the Clerk of the Bench position.[174] Cormack is described by Cook in another letter as a 'respectable free Emigrant'.[175] Two months later Cormack himself writes to the Post Master that he is too busy as he often spends a week in Port Stephens, a fortnight if a flood and that court related work has trebled since MacKay resigned. Cormack feels he could find someone in Dungog for the role if the salary were £30 a year.[176] A salary that Donald Campbell, the poundkeeper, is willing to accept according to Cook.[177]

Regardless of the salary paid, not all was satisfactory with the mails and in September 1837 Cook complained about the post service - Friday's letters arrive in Sydney the following Thursday and Tuesday's letters the following Monday, while special letters require the expense of being sent down to Raymond Terrace.[178] The postal service seemed to be in high demand and in November 1837 a total of £9/12/11 was taken in postage over three months.[179] In March the following year a joint complaint was made about the poor postal service, signed by Cormack and two others.[180] Complaints continued nevertheless and Cook was forced to declare that postal delays were not his fault.[181]

Another part of the administrative routine was the sending on of monies collected to Sydney. In October 1837 for example, £41/16/2 was paid to the Colonial Treasury and £2/10 to the Benevolent Society.[182] In the October quarter of the following year a total of £63/2/8 was collected in fines and £22/10/0 in fees.[183] Other routine matters for the Magistrate included advising Donald Campbell the poundkeeper that he needed to move closer to the pound or resign.[184] This was in response to a complaint by William Miller of Glen William to whom Cook wrote saying that Campbell had come to see him and promised to move.[185] Also routine were the applications by landholders for convicts, as in September 1837, when Cook needed to ask James Edward Ebsworth of Boorall to sit with him in a 'Special Petty Sessions' for this purpose.[186] Authorising ticket-of-leave men's transfers to other districts was another increasing part of a magistrate's role, with Cook reporting in the beginning of 1838 on the transfer of 11 men to various districts.[187]

Not so routine in the year 1838 was the drawing up of a Dungog town plan with allotments to be sold at auction. Cook was involved in the preparations for this, writing to the Colonial Secretary Thomson that no allotments had yet been sold in Dungog but a ready market would be found when 'properly defined and portioned off'.[188] In October that year, Cook received the 'plan for this township,' which he 'kept for the inspection of the Public'.[189]

Perhaps also routine but more exciting were escapes, as in August 1837 when Cook took a deposition on the escape of Thomas Ford, presumably before his mental problems arose, from two constables near 'Irish town of this District' while on his way to trial at the Supreme Court for cattle stealing. Cook had 'reason to believe' that drinking was involved, and with no handcuffs it was 'a very easy exit' for Ford. A man named Latham was now in the lock-up accused of being an accessory.[190] The constables responsible were 'Paterson Constables'.[191] Crimes such as cattle and horse stealing were also frequent, with for example, cattle slaughtered at Wallarobba being identified by Mr Chapman as his.[192] Assault was another common occurrence, and Charles White and Pat Brady were charged for 'assaulting and molesting John O'Brien at improper hours in his own house'.[193]

Escaping from custody was usually preceded by escape from one's place of assignment and so dealing with absconders and suspected absconders was also standard. When local landholder W. F. Forester declared that Margaret Sheedy was an absconder, and she that she was free, Margaret was held in custody while Cook determined the case.[194] Another was Thomas Mullins who, 'not giving a satisfactory account of himself,' was liable to be arrested as a vagrant.[195] In this case, Mullins was an absconder from Brisbane Water for which the constable who picked him up was rewarded £5.[196] This Constable Harcourt, who was 'free by servitude,' was still waiting for his reward to be paid three months later.[197] In the meantime Mullins escaped again. 'A more troublesome villain than Mullins I never did meet before now. The constable had a job of him.' This time Cook felt the 'right to claim the "Five Pounds" from the Constable and Gaoler who allowed him to escape'.[198]

For absconding and other crimes, punishment with the lash was often inflicted, as when William Forbes and William

Daley received 50 lashes each. John Ford was given 50 lashes plus 12 months on the 'Ironed gang' and John Cairns also 12 months.[199] Michael Welsh received 100 lashes for 'Cooking' sheep and cruelty to animals, and 12 months in an 'Ironed Gang' for absconding a second time.[200] William Evans, who dared to complain against his Master, a complaint Cook regarded as 'trifling and vexatious,' was given 50 lashes and returned.[201] Some exceptions were recognised however, as when Edward Birmingham was described as a simpleton who 'absconded through ignorance'.[202]

A more common punishment than the lash was to be deprived of ones ticket-of-leave. Both John Walsh and Harry Trowbridge lost their tickets-of-leave 'for improper treatment of Constable Powers when on duty on the Road between Stroud and Dungog'.[203] While William Dewhurst lost his as a warning to other overseers of the value of the flocks of the AAC. Dewhurst it seems was only able to be understood by George Jenkins who had been superintendent at the AAC for many years and Cook suggested that Dewhurst be sent to Liverpool Plains where Jenkins now was.[204] Loss of ticket-of-leave was a punishment that limited a person's mobility and thus made a servant of less use, as when J. M. Pilcher wrote to complain that his overseer Downs had been so punished. Cook reminded Pilcher that such a ticket was 'only to be enjoyed during good behaviour'.[205] Other technicalities associated with punishing a useful class of people was the need to inform the bench before trial that a master wanted a convict back, otherwise they would be sent to Sydney on conviction.[206]

The ticket-of-leave was a significant document and proof of right not to be arrested on the spot. Charles Romance claimed that his was lost when children in his hut took it from his coat pocket and destroyed it.[207] Lawrence Sullivan offered in pretence of his certificate of freedom what Cook described as a 'scrap of paper'.[208] Cook also felt he could accost anyone on the road and demand such proof, as he did of William Robissis 'on the Clarence Town Rd about 7 miles out'. When the reply was not satisfactory, he ordered him to appear before him in court.[209]

While dealing with convicts was naturally a significant part of a Police Magistrate's job, providing the Government with information was also significant, and so in 1837 Cook sent out a survey of both Upper Williams and Port Stephens requesting information on the average wages of 'mechanics' and prices in the district for the six months to 30th June.[210] The major landowners he sent this to in Dungog were, James Marshall, C. L. Brown, W. H. Windyer, James Walker, Lowe, D. F. MacKay, John Hooke, J. Forester, Myles, E. Ross, Barrymore, Meyer, and Holmes. The information was returned and complied by the beginning of November and included average wages, with and without board and lodging, numbers required in addition to those already employed and average prices. Overall, Dungog was a more expensive place than Port Stephens but paid higher wages.[211]

Return showing the average Prices of Provisions and Agricultural Produce in the District of the Upper Williams for the Six Months until 30th June 1837

Articles	**Average Prices**
Maize	3/6 - 4/ bushel
Wheat	6/6 - 7/ bushel
(Indian) Corn	3 - 4½ lb
Beef	3½ - 4 lb
Pork	6 - 7 lb
Mutton	6 lb
Tea	3/ - 4/ lb
Sugar	6/ lb
Tobacco	3/6 - 4/ lb
Butter	1/6 - 2/ lb

Cheese	6 ?
Milk	3 quart

NB When the Settlers here supply their free servants with groceries - they usually charge twenty five percent on the Sydney prices.

Return showing the average Prices of Provisions and Agricultural Produce in the District of Port Stephens for the Six Months until 30th June 1837

Articles	**Average Prices**
Maize	2/6 - 4/ bushel
Wheat	4/ - 9/ bushel
Barley	4/ - 5/ bushel
Tobacco	2 - 3 lb
Lemons, Potatoes & every vegetable	½ - 1 lb
Flour, Fine	2½ - 3½ lb
Flour, Seconds	2 - 3 lb
Beef	4 - 5 lb
Mutton	4 - 5 lb
Pork	6 - 8 lb
Tea	2/6 - 3/ lb
Sugar	6 - 7 lb
Salt	1½ lb
Soap	6 - 7 lb
Cheese	6 lb
Butter	1 - 1/6 lb
Talcom	4 - 5 lb
Hogs lark	6 - 8 lb
Lamp oil	3 - 3/6 gal
Rum	16/ gal
Wine (cup?)	5/ -/8/

Return Showing the Average Prices of Provisions and Agricultural Produce in the District of the Upper Williams for the six months ended 30 June 1837.

Articles	Average Prices		
Maize	3/6	@	4/ bus
Wheat	6/6	@	7/
Flour	3d	@	3½d lb
Beef	3½	@	6
Pork	6	@	7
Mutton	—	—	6
Tea	3/	@	4/
Sugar	—	—	6
Tobacco	3/6	@	4/
Butter	1/6	@	2/
Cheese	—	—	6
Milk	—	—	8d quart

(Signed) Thos. Cook JP
Col. Mag.

N.B. When the settlers have supplied their free servants with groceries — they usually charge twenty five per cent on the Sydney price.

continued forward

Return showing the average Wages of Mechanics & Others in the District of Upper Williams
for the Six Months until 30th June 1837 and the numbers required in addition to those already employed

Trade	**Average Wages per day without B&L**	**Per Annum with B&L**	**Number required**
Carpenter & Joiner (rough)	4/ - 5/	£40 - 50	15
Cabinet Maker	6/ -7/	£70 - 80	5
Blacksmith & Farrier	6/ -7/	£70 - 80	6
Wheel Wright	7/	£80	4
Cooper	4/6 - 5/	£40 - 50	2
Stone Mason	5/ - 6/	£60 - 70	5
Brick Maker	5/ - 6/	£60 - 70	4
Sawyer	5/ - 6/	£60 - 70	10
Fencer & Splitter	4/6 - 5/	£40 - 50	0
Shoemaker	4/	£40 - 45	5
Taylor	4/6 - 5/	£40 - 50	2
Nailor	5/ - 6/	£60 - 70	1
Plasterer	6/ - 7/	£70 - 80	5
Turner ?			2
Harness Maker			1
Shepherds	3/6 -	£30 - 35	12
Laborers of all sorts	3/ - 3/6	£25 - 30	150

Return showing the average Wages of Mechanics & Others in the District of Port Stephens
for the Six Months until 30th June 1837 and the numbers required in addition to those already employed (allowance for B&L 10/- 12/- per week)

Trade or Calling	Average Wages per day without B&L	Per Annum with B&L	Number required
Builder	about 6/5	£100	
Carpenter & Joiner	about 1/11	£35 - 35	4
Bricklayer & Plasterers	about 3/10	£60	2
Saddler & Harness Maker	about 2/7	£40	1
Blacksmith	about 3/10	£60	1
Farrier			1
Shipwright	3/2 -	£50	
Brickmakers	1/	£15 - 20	
Sawyers	are generally paid by the price 7/6 per 100 feet sawn timber		
Bullock drives and shepherds	1/ -1/6/	£20 - 25	
Laborers	1/ -1/6/	£20 - 25	

At the beginning of 1838, another return was required, this time concerning an 'estimate of Agricultural Produce'. One flour mill and one threshing machine was reported in the Upper Williams district and one mill and two threshers in the AAC lands, but no quarries or mines.[212]

While the government favoured information on mills and mines, a glimpse into the social and even economic networks of those who would operate outside the law as upheld by Police Magistrate Thomas Cook is seen in his account of the activities of Thomas Ford. Ford had been recaptured and while free had been selling and branding cattle 'for the purpose of raising money and deceiving government'. Ford had made contact with a Dark of Hinton who had borrowed money from Andrew Lang of Paterson. Phillip O'Brien was the principle purchaser of cattle, and one of Hooke's had been killed and six others stamped over 10-12 days according to witness James Doherty. Ford and partner Latham had bought casks off William Miller to cure four tons of beef. Thomas Bamford was their cooper employed to seal the casks, whereabouts unknown. Ford had a witness on his behalf, a Robert Hassratha?, and a friend of Darks.[213]

In addition to cattle stealing, another common crime was forgery, as when Patrick Brenan, alias Maccurran, forged a draft for £13/15 on 'Mr Lord of Sydney' and a local landowner. Brenan, attempted to cash the draft at O'Brien's store near Clarence Town. The draft was supposedly drawn by Lord's superintendent Mr Flitt. O'Brien called on Mr Flitt to check and so the forgery was discovered. A warrant for Brenan's arrest was issued by another landowning JP, Lawrence Myles, in Cook's absence.[214]

Landowners such as Lord and Myles also needed to abide by the restrictions on their workers, and at the end of 1837 Cook reminded John Hooke that application must be made to the superintendent of convicts before 'your man' could leave the District, as Hooke proposed.[215] Cook also queried matters between landowners that he felt were not legal, as when this same John Hooke purchased the property of Lawrence Myles, including all his assigned servants. Cook wrote for advice on the legality of this to the Commissioner for the Assignment of Servants.[216] This was a case that would continue for some time and in the following month, Cook wrote to Myles pointing out that the 'alienation of his Wallarobba meadow' had not been reported and that he needed to see the assignment regulations.[217] At the same time, Cook wrote to Hooke, the purchaser of this Wallarobba meadow, to point out 'an apparent irregularity in the construction of your present establishment as regards some convict servants'. He requested that Hooke 'without delay turn to the 15th paragraph of the assignment regulations.'[218]

Despite Cook's (seemingly prescient) disquiet, the transfer of both land and convicts from Myles to Hooke went ahead and Cook was reduced to overseeing the details. He wrote to Hooke to insist that the appropriate forms be filled in, particularly all servants' names.[219] Cook informed J. M. Slade, Superintendent of Convicts, that Hooke had complied and Myles not, but that the transfer would go ahead anyway.[220] A couple of days later Myles wrote with the list of convicts, 24 in total, including such names as William Mumford (*Lady MacNaughton*), John Farrell (*Clyde*) and John Pritchard (*Printra*), to complete the transfer of property and servants to 'John Hooke of Wiragully Farm'.[221] The Wallarobba Meadow property under question consisted of four lots of 2,560/790/640 and 940 acres, and 25 men.[222]

Despite these formalities, the following year this transaction took an unexpected turn when Hooke swore that Myles and MacKay had entered into a conspiracy to deprive him of one of the convicts, a John Lingfoot. Cook was obliged to write to Slade asking him to check the original list of convicts that was to be transferred, as Lingfoot was not on the copy Cook had.[223] A few days later Cook appears to have accepted Hooke's claims, reporting that 'the name Lingfoot has been by some Chicanery withdrawn from this list,' and that Lingfoot had joined his 'former master' Myles in Sydney.[224]

While Cook was making great efforts in the Myles/Hooke land deal, at around the same time occurred an incident that shows surprising limits to the authority of the Police Magistrate, at least in dealings that concerned the native people. Cook had to write to 'The Hon E. Deas Thomson,' the Colonial Secretary, seeking advice in how to proceed in a 'case of native wives being detained against their will and that of their friends'. After a 'formal complaint by a respectable person' was made in favour of five aboriginals, Cook interviewed the five 'blacks,' including Fullam Derby and Pirrson, who he described as 'most intelligent fellows,' and that 'Derby is a king and speaks English well'. Cook discovered that the superintendent of Mr John Lord, Mr Flitt, had detained their wives, in fact that he 'keeps quite a seraglio'. Cook sent a note to Flitt 'via one of the blacks,' only to have them report back that Flitt had torn it to pieces. Cook wrote that he 'feared ill blood and foul murder may result,' and requested 'instructions how to proceed'.[225] While the results of this case are unknown, it is apparent that Flitt's arrest was not one.

While Cook may have felt frustrated at his lack of control over people such as Mr Flitt, in another area he certainly displayed more energy. Cook was concerned that absconding convicts were easily able to obtain work among an increasing population of either ex-convicts or simply people anxious to obtain a worker and not keen to ask too many questions. As Cook described an absconder from his own property named Joseph Ailkens, he is 'a sort of rough carpenter and being a plausible fellow will easily find employment'.[226] This concern grew as settlement on the Peel River to the north opened up new opportunities for employment far from authority. Cook wrote in May 1835 of five absconders from AAC lands who, once past Maitland, hoped to find employment on the Peel. Cook suggested mounted police to recapture them and a fine for any that employed them.[227]

In July 1838 Cook emphasised the point that settlers too easily assisted runaways by detailing the case of Pat Brady (alias Brown) who absconded in December 1836, taking a steamer to Sydney (presumably paying with money he should not have had), from where he walked to Parramatta.

Here he took up with a party being taken down to Port Philip, being paid £3. He then returned to the Hunter region and took a contract with Mr Dawson of Black Creek as a shepherd for £22 and a large ration 'without anything to show for his freedom'.[228]

Cook would have been pleased when in the following October he was able to summons 'a Mr MacKay for harbouring & employing 2 convicts illegally at large,' namely Bing Petty and John Smith.[229] However, continuing frustration over this issue is expressed soon after when Cook wrote that 'Bushranger is merely a prettier name for "High Wayman" ' and complained again of people 'harbouring & employing'.[230] The crack down in this area continued, and in November at least three people were fined substantially for 'harbouring & employing': R. B. Dawson of Black Creek – £224.14.4; Alex McLeod – £112.9.8 and Alex L. Dave – £112.9.8.[231]

While Cook throughout the letters shows some sympathy on occasion for others, he had the limitations of his times. When his servant John Flynn died in hospital, Cook applied to the Commissioner of Assignment to send another, in 'stout health' and 'one that can eat his bread and earn it'. Cook declared that as he had 40 acres cleared he was entitled.[232] The next day Cook wrote to the Superintendent of Convicts to inform him that John Flynn had had an accident 'on my farm' in early February and had died.[233]

The Dungog Magistrate's Letterbook ends in early 1839 as it began, with routine matters, such as fines being sent to the Benevolent Institution and a deposition being taken in a robbery case.[234] Also at the beginning of 1839, Thomas Cook, writing from his estate, Auchentorlie near Dungog, took the 'oath of allegiance' and so was prepared to continue in his position. This he does until cost cutting in 1843-44 sees him acting as an unpaid magistrate just as any landowning Justice of the Peace such as John Hooke and others he has dealt with.[235]

The Letterbook is scattered throughout with the names of members of this anomalous community. In addition to the Police Magistrate Thomas Cook himself, there are those of landowners and grantees, names that are also known from other sources, such as Myles, Hooke, MacKay, Mackenzie, Lord, and Brown; names that even now appear on the street signs of Dungog town today. There are also the names of various workers within the system, Clerks of the Bench D. F. MacKay and William Cormack, also known elsewhere, and of others less well known or known only in these pages - the pound keepers, William Spencer at Paterson and Donald Campbell at Dungog, watch house keepers, John McGibbon and James Boland at Dungog, and Alexander Hamilton at Stroud. Not to be neglected are the many ex-convict enforcers of the law, constables such as Michael Connolly at Dungog, John Tippary and Patrick Conway at Gloucester, and James Edwards and Robert Mason of Stroud, and of course the scourger John Powers, also of Stroud. Naturally, there appeared before the Dungog Magistrate many convicts, such as the patient escapee Thomas Fogarty, the nervously afflicted Thomas Ford, the 'troublesome villain' Thomas Mullins and the much desired John Lingfoot, most of whom, if they survived, would have eventually become 'free by servitude'. Also appearing in these letters are the names, even if they are sometimes names of foreign origin, of the original inhabitants of the Williams valley, of Fulham Derby, McAuthy, Jemmi and Kotra Jacki, witnesses to, victims of and players in, the great changes influencing and destroying their society as the anomalous community glimpsed in this Letterbook establishes itself.

Perhaps no single letter in the Dungog Police Magistrate's Letterbook tells us something not previously known about this period of colonial history. But taken in its entirety the Letterbook provides a fascinating snapshot of this early handful of years at a time when magistrates were required to deal with a wide range of matters within a community that Thomas Cook quite rightly describes as 'anomalous'.

[1] The first of these letterbooks is the Magistrates' Letterbook for the police districts of Dungog and Port Stephens, New South Wales, 1834-1839, a manuscript held by the National Library of Australia - MS 3550. See below *This anomalous community*, p.xx. The bulk of the letterbooks, running until 1851, are held in the NSW State Archives - SRNSW: NRS 2965. That the letterbook in the NLA was in fact part of this longer series was only pointed out by the author in 2011.

[2] *Sydney Gazette*, 31/3/1838, p.2.

[3] Magistrates' Letterbook, Dungog, various letters.

[4] *The Sydney Herald*, 9/9/1839, p.2.

[5] Magistrates' Letterbook, Dungog: Cook to Colonial Storekeeper, 13/3/1837 & Cook to Thomson, 14/12/1837.

[6] NSW Death Certificate, Thomas Cook, No. 1866/002181 & *Sydney Gazette*, 5/4/1834, p.2.

[7] *Sydney Herald*, 17/11/1834, p.4.

[8] *The Australian*, 9/12/1834, p.2. See also *Sydney Morning Herald*, 8/6/1874, p.1.

[9] *Sydney Herald*, 8/10/1835, p.2. Magistrate Thomas Cook is sometimes mistakenly credited with having 'named' Dungog, but this had officially occurred before even his arrival in the Colony.

[10] *The Sydney Herald*, 1/6/1835, p.2.

[11] *Sydney Gazette*, **16/11/1839, p.4, Report of the Committee on Police and Gaols.**

[12] *Sydney Morning Herald*, 12/2/1866, p.1 and 6/9/1871, p.8.

[13] *Sydney Herald*, 7/12/1841, p.2.

[14] *The Colonist*, 8/6/1837, p.3.

[15] *Australasian Chronicle*, 31/3/1840, p.2. [*The Australasian Chronicle* was a pro-Catholic paper edited at that time by a Scottish convert to Catholicism, William Augustine Duncan.]

[16] *Australasian Chronicle*, 31/3/1840, p.2.

[17] *Australasian Chronicle*, 3/4/1840, p.2.

[18] *The Sydney Monitor and Commercial Advertiser*, 6/4/1840, p.3S

[19] *Australasian Chronicle*, 21/4/1840, p.2.

[20] *Sydney Herald*, 11/5/1840, p.1S.

[21] *Sydney Herald*, 11/5/1840, p.1S.

[22] *Australasian Chronicle*, 14/4/1840, p.2, & 12/5/1840, p.2.

[23] *Sydney Herald*, 22/5/1840, p.2.

[24] *Australasian Chronicle*, 26/5/1840, p.2.

[25] *Australasian Chronicle*, 29/5/1840, p.2.

[26] SRNSW: NRS 2965, 4/5539-40, 2/8210 2, Thomas Cook to John Hooke, 24/4/1840.
[27] *Australasian Chronicle*, 25/6/1840, p.2.
[28] SRNSW: NRS 2965, [4/5539-40, 2/8210 2], Thomas Cook to Michael Ryan, 5/5/1840.
[29] *Australasian Chronicle*, 21/7/1840, p.2.
[30] *Australasian Chronicle*, 20/8/1840, p.3.
[31] *Australasian Chronicle*, 5/9/1840, p.2.
[32] SRNSW: NRS 2965, [4/5539-40, 2/8210 2], Thomas Cook to Attorney-General, 14/9/1840.
[33] *Australasian Chronicle*, 22/10/1840, p.2. This notice was repeated in several following editions.
[34] *Sydney Gazette*, 5/11/1840, p.2.
[35] *Australasian Chronicle*, 26/12/1840, p.2.
[36] *Australasian Chronicle*, 18/9/1841, p.2.
[37] *Sydney Herald*, 28/1/1841, p.3, & 2/2/1841, p.3.
[38] *Sydney Herald*, 18/5/1841, p.2.
[39] *Australasian Chronicle*, 21/2/1843, p.3, & *Maitland Mercury*, 1/4/1843, p.2.
[40] *Sydney Herald*, 13/11/1839, p.1S.
[41] *Sydney Herald*, 13/11/1839, p.1S.
[42] *Maitland Mercury*, 19/3/1844, p.S1.
[43] *Maitland Mercury*, 28/6/1845, p.3.
[44] *Sydney Morning Herald*, 16/6/1845, p.1; *Maitland Mercury*, 28/6/1845, p.3.
[45] *Morning Chronicle*, 5/7/1845, p.2.
[46] This was presumably after Auchentorlie House located in the district of Paisley in Renfrewshire, Scotland.
[47] *NSW Government Gazette*, Oct 1839, pp.1159-1160.
[48] *Maitland Mercury*, 25/2/1846, p.4; 18/11/1846, p.2; 21/10/1846, p.2; 3/11/1849, p.4.
[49] *Sydney Morning Herald*, 12/3/1844, p.3; *Maitland Mercury*, 16/2/1848, p.2, & *Maitland Mercury*, 5/9/1846, p.2.
[50] *Maitland Mercury*, 16/5/1849, p.4; 23/7/1853, p.4.
[51] *Maitland Mercury*, 9/8/1851, p.3.
[52] *Sydney Morning Herald*, 12/12/1851, p.2; *Maitland Mercury*, 29/3/1854, p.4.
[53] *Sydney Morning Herald*, 16/10/1845, p.3.
[54] *Maitland Mercury*, 12/2/1848, p.2.
[55] *Maitland Mercury*, 15/11/1848, p.2.
[56] *Maitland Mercury*, 3/2/1849, p.3.
[57] *Maitland Mercury*, 18/10/1854, p.2.
[58] *The Colonist*, 20/10/1836, p.7.

[59] *Sydney Morning Herald*, 21/11/1842, p.3 and *Maitland Mercury*, 29/5/1852, p.2.

[60] *Sydney Morning Herald*, 8/6/1874, p.1.

[61] *Maitland Mercury*, 21/3/1855, p.1S. (Now known as the Crimean War.)

[62] *Maitland Mercury*, 5/9/1855, p.2.

[63] *Maitland Mercury*, 22/9/1855, p.2. The Free Church of Scotland was formed after the 'Disruption of 1843' when 450 ministers of the established Church of Scotland broke away over the issue of the Church's relationship with the State.

[64] *Maitland Mercury*, 8/5/1856, p.4.

[65] *Maitland Mercury*, 4/10/1854, p.2.

[66] *Maitland Mercury*, 2/10/1856, p.4.

[67] Votes & Proceedings of NSW Legislative Assembly, 25/8/1857, 'Thomas Abbott, Late Chief Constable at Dungog'. *Maitland Mercury*, 2/10/1856, p.4.

[68] *Maitland Mercury*, 14/2/1857, p.7S.

[69] *Sydney Morning Herald*, 3/2/1857, p.1; 7/2/1857, p.3.

[70] *Maitland Mercury*, 11/9/1858, p.1.

[71] *Maitland Mercury*, 13/4/1858, p.3.

[72] *Maitland Mercury*, 3/9/1857, p.2; 26/8/1858, p.3; 7/9/1858, p.3; 25/9/1858, p.1 & 14/10/1858, p.3.

[73] *Maitland Mercury*, 17/5/1859, p.4.

[74] *Sydney Morning Herald*, 12/2/1863, p.5

[75] *Sydney Morning Herald*, 31/7/1863, p.4.

[76] *Maitland Mercury*, 30/7/1864, p.2.

[77] *Sydney Morning Herald*, 12/2/1866, p.1.

[78] *Sydney Morning Herald*, 9/4/1870, p.4.

[79] *Sydney Morning Herald*, 6/9/1871, p.8.

[80] *Daily Mirror*, 8/12/1981.

[81] Maurie Garland, *The Trials of Isabelle Mary Kelly*, p.74.

[82] Cook is referred to by "Urbanus" writing from Berrima as "the Buffoon Cook, (or Captain Cook, as he has dubbed himself without commission in army or navy, since his elevation from the spinning jenny at Manchester to the Australian bench)". *Australasian Chronicle*, 7/4/1840, p.2.

[83] A version of this paper first appeared in the *Journal of the Royal Australian Historical Society*, 108(1), p.73.

[84] Magistrates' Letterbook for the police districts of Dungog and Port Stephens, New South Wales, 1834-1839. (Manuscript, National Library of Australia.) Dungog is on the Williams River, which flows into the Hunter at Raymond Terrace and is above the head of navigation at Clarence Town. Land grants had commenced along the Williams by 1829. All references are to the Letterbook unless stated otherwise.

[85] All these examples are discussed below.

[86] Cook to Principle Superintendent of Convicts, 15/11/1837.

[87] These examples are to be found throughout the Letterbook.

[88] Cook to Pilcher, 1/10/1837.

[89] For example, Cook to Slade, Super of Convicts, 19/3/1838. This case is discussed in detail below.

[90] For example, Cook to Hon E Deas Thomson, Colonial Secretary, 23/7/1838.

[91] *Sydney Gazette*, 16/11/1839, p.4, 'Report of the Committee on Police and Gaols'.

[92] Cook to Ebswoth, 9/11/1838 (John Williams), Cook to Colonial Secretary, 6/6/1838 (Mrs Parker), & Cook to Thomson, 14/12/1837 (Fullam Derby).

[93] These cases are referred to below.

[94] Moffitt to Colonial Secretary, 3/1/1834.

[95] Moffitt to Colonial Secretary, 31/1/1834.

[96] Moffatt to Mackenzie, 7/3/1834.

[97] Mackenzie to Colonial Secretary, 4/4/1834.

[98] Mackenzie to William Dun, Coroner, Paterson, 15/4/1834.

[99] MacKay to Major Croker, Officer Commanding, Paterson, 2/7/1835.

[100] MacKay to Paterson Magistrate, 21/1/1835. (See also *Government Gazette*, 30/5/1835 & 15/7/1835.)

[101] MacKay to Attorney-General, 26/2/1836.

[102] Myles to Lieutenant Beckham, Commander Mounted Police, Jerry's Plains, 20/5/1836.

[103] Mackenzie to George Brooks, Newcastle, 14/7/1834.

[104] Cook to Attorney-General, 24/7/1835 & 8/8/1835.

[105] Mackenzie to Colonial Secretary, 18/9/1834.

[106] Cook to Police Magistrate, Paterson, 25/8/1838.

[107] Cook to E. Deas Thomson, 8/2/1839.

[108] Cook to E. Deas Thomson, 26/10/1837.

[109] Mackenzie to Colonial Secretary, 16/4/1834.

[110] *Sydney Gazette*, 16/11/1839, p.4.

[111] Thomas Cook, his wife and several children arrived in Sydney in April 1834, he took oath as a magistrate in November that year, and became the Police Magistrate of Port Stephens from which he visited Dungog (*Sydney Gazette*, 5/4/1834, p.2; *Sydney Herald*, 20/11/1834, p.3 & 15/11/1834, p.4). Soon after this the police districts were reorganised and in 1837 Cook was appointed Police Magistrate of both Upper Williams and Port Stephens, but residing at Dungog and now visiting Stroud. Most of what is known of Thomas Cook comes from a period after the end of the Letterbook. While at Dungog Cook purchased a property that he named 'Auchentorlie'. Cook lost his position as Police Magistrate in 1843 when the government reverted to unpaid magistrates, but he continued serving as a Justice of the Peace. He also lost both a daughter and a son to illness while living at Dungog (*Sydney Morning Herald*, 21/11/1842, p.3 & *Maitland Mercury*, 2/6/1852, p.3). In the 1850's, Cook sold Auchentorlie and left Dungog, dying at Woollahra in 1866 (*Sydney Morning Herald*, 12/2/1866, p.1).

[112] Cook to E. Deas Thomson, 18/6/1838.

[113] Cook to Police Magistrate, Paterson, 21/9/1837.

[114] Cook to Superintendent of Convicts, 27/12/1834.

[115] Cook to Alexander McLeay, 19/5/1835.

[116] Cook to Superintendent of Convicts, 6/5/1835.

[117] Cook to Officer Commanding Mounted Police, Maitland, 29/1/1836.

[118] MacKay to Francis Fisher, Crown Solicitor, 3/9/1836.

[119] MacKay to McPherson, Collector of Internal Revenue, 20/8/1836. The original 'River William' gradually became 'Williams' River' and finally as now, the 'Williams River'.

[120] Cook to Johnston, Superintendent of Police, Newcastle, 31/8/1836. The census was 2/9/1836.

[121] Cook to Holden, Government House, 7/10/1836.

[122] Cook to Superintendent of Police, Newcastle, 16/12/1836.

[123] Cook to John Ryan Brennan, 26/4/1837.

[124] Cook to Bench of Magistrates, Newcastle, 26/9/1838.

[125] Cook to W. W. Lewis, Colonial Architect, 28/2/1837.

[126] Cook to Commissioner for AAC, 2/8/1837.

[127] Cook to Colonial Secretary, 26/4/1837 and 2/8/1837.

[128] Cook to Attorney-General, 16/9/1837 and 25/10/1837.

[129] Cook to Superintendent of Convicts, Major of Brigade, & Colonial Storekeeper, 3/3/1837.

[130] Cook to Colonial Storekeeper, 2/12/1837.

[131] Cook to Colonial Secretary, 13/3/1837.

[132] Cook to Colonial Secretary, 13/3/1837.

[133] Cook to Colonial Storekeeper, 27/3/1837.

[134] Cook to Commissioner for Assignment of Servants, 26/10/1837.

[135] Cook to Colonial Secretary, Return re: blankets and Aboriginal numbers, 1/8/1837.
[136] Cook to Colonial Storekeeper, 26/3/1838, 9/1/1839.
[137] Cook to Colonial Secretary, 31/12/1838.
[138] Cook to Commissioner for AAC, 10/8/1837.
[139] Cook to Colonial Secretary, 9/9/1837.
[140] Cook to Colonial Secretary, 27/3/1837.
[141] Cook to Colonial Secretary, 8/8/1837.
[142] Cook to Commissioner for AAC, 18/7/1837 & 19/7/1837.
[143] Cook to William Dun, 10/8/1837.
[144] Cook to William Dun, 18/8/1837.
[145] Cook to Ebsworth, 6/10/1837.
[146] Cook to Colonial Secretary, 25/4/1838.
[147] Cook to Colonial Secretary, 22/7/1837.
[148] Cook to Colonial Secretary, 3/7/1837.
[149] Cook to William Lithgow, Auditor-General, 15/7/1837.
[150] Cook to William Lithgow, Auditor-General, 3/7/1837.
[151] Cook to Dumaresq, Commissioner for AAC, 11/10/1837.
[152] Cook to Colonial Secretary, 15/7/1837.
[153] Cook to Colonial Secretary, 10/8/1838.
[154] Cook to AAC, 10/8/1837.
[155] Cook to Johnston, 28/11/1838.
[156] Cook to AAC, 17/8/1837.
[157] Cook to Colonial Secretary, 30/9/1837.
[158] Cook to Colonial Secretary, 30/9/1837.
[159] Cook to Dumaresq, 22/11/1837.
[160] Cook to Thomson, 5/12/1837.
[161] Cook to Smith, 5/3/1838.
[162] Cook to Colonial Secretary, 30/8/1837.
[163] Cook to Police Magistrate, Illawarra, 11/10/1837.
[164] State Archives, Colonial Secretary's Correspondence, reel 2812: Colonial Secretary to Police Magistrate, Dungog, 18/10/1837.
[165] Cook to Colonial Secretary, 18/8/1837.
[166] Cook to Colonial Secretary, 16/8/1837.
[167] Cook to Colonial Secretary, 16/8/1837.
[168] Cook to Park, 23/2/1838.
[169] Cook to Alexander Livingston, 5/3/1838.
[170] Cook to Colonial Secretary, 14/11/1838.
[171] Cook to Colonial Surgeon, 1/2/1839.
[172] Cook to Colonial Secretary, 9/2/1839.
[173] Cook to Colonial Secretary, 6/6/1838.
[174] MacKay to Post Master, 10/7/1837.
[175] Cook to Colonial Secretary, 16/9/1837.

[176] Cormack to Post Master, 15/9/1837.
[177] Cook to Colonial Secretary, 26/9/1837.
[178] Cook to Colonial Secretary, 26/9/1837.
[179] Cormack to Post Master, 23/11/1837.
[180] Cormack, Sullivan, Warn to Post Master, 17/3/1838.
[181] Cook to Colonel Lacy, 30/7/1838.
[182] Cook to Colonial Treasury, 27/10/1837, Cool to Richard Jones, 26/10/1837.
[183] Cormack to Colonial Secretary, 1/1/1838.
[184] Cook to Campbell, 24/8/1837.
[185] Cook to Miller, 25/8/1837.
[186] Cook to Edwards, 30/8/1837.
[187] Cook to Superintendent of Convicts, 21/1/1838.
[188] Cook to Colonial Secretary, 17/3/1838.
[189] Cook to Colonel Lucy, 27/10/1838.
[190] Cook to Colonial Secretary, 24/8/1837.
[191] Cook to Attorney-General, 26/8/1837.
[192] Cook to Colonial Secretary, 25/8/1838 & 17/9/1838.
[193] Cook to Colonial Secretary, 6/10/1838.
[194] Cook to Superintendent of Convicts, John McLean, 17/10/1837.
[195] Cook to Paterson Bench, 31/8/1837.
[196] Cook to Colonial Secretary, 17/9/1837.
[197] Cook to Colonial Secretary, 12/12/1837.
[198] Cook to Henry Denin, Brisbane Waters, 5/1/1837.
[199] Cook to Colonial Secretary, 21/9/1837.
[200] Cook to Colonial Secretary, 1210/1837.
[201] Cook to Police Magistrate, Maitland, 24/11/1838.
[202] Cook to Colonial Secretary, 21/9/1837.
[203] Cook to Cormack, 23/11/1837.
[204] Cook to Superintendent of Convicts, 2/12/1837.
[205] Cook to Pilcher, 1/10/1837.
[206] Cook to Ebsworth, 8/6/1838.
[207] Cook to Superintendent of Convicts, 11/7/1838.
[208] Cook to Superintendent of Convicts, 31/1/1839.
[209] Cook to Police Magistrate, Paterson, 26/1/1839.
[210] Cook to Colonial Secretary, 3/10/1837.
[211] Letterbook copy of returns, November 1837.
[212] Cook to Colonial Secretary, 12/1/1838.
[213] Cook to Colonial Secretary, 17/10/1837.
[214] Cook to Colonial Secretary, 1/11/1837.
[215] Cook to Hooke, 23/11/1837.
[216] Cook to Commissioner for the Assignment of Servants, 26/10/1837.
[217] Cook to Myles, 22/12/1837.

[218] Cook to Hooke, 22/12/1837.
[219] Cook to Hooke, 22/12/1837.
[220] Cook to Slade, 16/1/1838.
[221] Lawrence Myles to Police magistrate, 18/12/1837. [This is the only example in the book of a copy of a letter addressed to the Dungog court rather than being as all others, an outwards letter.]
[222] Cook to Colonial Secretary, 19/12/1837.
[223] Cook to Superintendent of Convicts, 17/3/1838.
[224] Cook to Superintendent of Convicts, 21/3/1838.
[225] Cook to Thomson, 14/12/1837.
[226] Cook to Superintendent of Convicts, 19/12/1837.
[227] Cook to Colonial Secretary, 26/5/1838.
[228] Cook to Colonial Secretary, 23/7/1838.
[229] Cook to Police Magistrate, Paterson, 8/10/1838.
[230] Cook to Colonial Secretary, 20/10/1838.
[231] Cook to Clerk of the Peace, 24/11/1838.
[232] Cook to Commissioner of Assignment, 2/3/1838.
[233] Cook to Superintendent of Convicts, 3/3/1838.
[234] Cook to Colonial Secretary, 9/2/1839, 2/3/1839.
[235] Cook to Colonial Secretary, 9/2/1839.

About the author

Michael Williams is an historian of local Australia and of the Chinese Diaspora. His dissertation at the University of Hong Kong employed oral history and archival research to examine the links of the villages of the Pearl River Delta with the Pacific Ports of Sydney, Hawaii and San Francisco. He is a founding member of the Chinese Australian Historical Society. Michael also lived for many years in the rural NSW town of Dungog where he did much local history research into this lovely and fascinating town.

Publisher of many academic papers and books, Michael seeks to make his research more widely available outside university firewalls and at a lower cost.

www.ingramcontent.com/pod-product-compliance
Lightning Source LLC
LaVergne TN
LVHW050343160826
845677LV00014B/3769